WHAT IS A
MONARCHY?

MARGARET R. MEAD

Crabtree Publishing Company
www.crabtreebooks.com

Crabtree Publishing Company

www.crabtreebooks.com

Produced and developed by Netscribes Inc.

Author: Margaret R. Mead
Publishing plan research and development:
Sean Charlebois, Reagan Miller
Crabtree Publishing Company
Editors: Valerie J. Weber, Lynn Peppas
Proofreaders: Wendy Scavuzzo, Sarah Chasse
Art director: Dibakar Acharjee
Picture researcher: Sandeep Kumar Guthikonda
Project coordinator: Kathy Middleton
Print coordinator: Katherine Berti
Production coordinator: Kenneth J. Wright
Prepress technician: Kenneth J. Wright
Cover design: Margaret Amy Salter, Katherine Berti

Front cover: Painting of Queen Victoria of England wearing crown
and coronation robes; Buckingham Palace Garden (background);
Prince Albert II of Monaco (inset top); Emperor Jinmu (inset
bottom)

Title page: King Henry VII of England

Photographs:
Title page: Duncan Walker/istockphoto; P4: GYI NSEA/
EdStock/istockphoto; P5: John Stillwell-Pool/Getty Images; P6:
Renata Sedmakova /Shutterstock; P7: Featureflash / Shutterstock;
P8-9: Mart/Shutterstock; P10: Yiannis Papadimitriou/ Shutterstock;
P11: Gianni Dagli Orti/Corbis; P12: Bettmann/ CORBIS; P13:
Hulton Archive/Stringer/Gettyimages; P14: Alfredo Dagli Orti/The
Art Archive/Corbis; P15: Bettmann/CORBIS; P16: 1000 Words /
Shutterstock; P17: mbonaparte/Shutterstock; P18: Jinty Jackson/
AFP/Getty Images; P19: Nicku/Shutterstock; P20: PABALLO
THEKISO/AFP/Getty Images; P21: David Ramos/Getty Images;
P22: Chris Jackson-WPA Pool/Getty Images; P23: Pablo Blazquez
Dominguez/ WireImage/ Gettyimages; P24: imagemaker /
Shutterstock; P25: Anwar Hussein/Getty Images; P26: Chris
Jackson/Getty Images; P27: CHAFIK/AFP/Getty Images; P28:
iconspro/Shutterstock; P29: Bjorn Stefanson/Shutterstock; P30:
Zurijeta/Shutterstock; P31: ALLAN MILLIGAN/AFP/Getty
Images; P32: RuthChoi/Shutterstock; P33: ALEXANDRA
JONES/AFP/Getty Images; P34: Popperfoto/Getty Images; P35:
NICOLAS LAMBERT/AFP/Getty Images; P36: vichie81/
Shutterstock; P37: AHMAD FAIZAL YAHYA / Shutterstock; P40:
CHRISTOPHE ARCHAMBAULT/AFP/Getty Images; P41.1:
dutourdumonde / Shutterstock; P41.2: Mr Pics / Shutterstock; P42:
ChameleonsEye/Shutterstock; P43: Ricardo Esplana Babor /
Shutterstock; P44: Renata Sedmakova/ Shutterstock; P45: John
Rogers Herbert/The Bridgeman Art Library/Gettyimages.
Thinkstock: front cover (left); Shutterstock: front cover
(background); Shutterstock/Featureflash: front cover (inset top);
Wikimedia Commons/Gink Adachi: front cover (inset bottom)

Library and Archives Canada Cataloguing in Publication

Mead, Margaret R.
What is a monarchy? / Margaret R. Mead.

(Forms of government)
Includes index.
Issued also in electronic format.
ISBN 978-0-7787-5318-6 (bound).--ISBN 978-0-7787-5325-4 (pbk.)

1. Monarchy--Juvenile literature. I. Title. II. Series: Forms
of government (St. Catharines, Ont.)

JC375.M42 2013   j321'.6   C2013-901192-7

Library of Congress Cataloging-in-Publication Data

Mead, Margaret R.
What is a monarchy? / Margaret R. Mead.
pages cm. -- (Forms of government)
Includes index.
ISBN 978-0-7787-5318-6 (reinforced library binding) --
ISBN 978-0-7787-5325-4 (pbk.) -- ISBN 978-1-4271-8789-5
(electronic pdf.) -- ISBN 978-1-4271-9627-9 (electronic html.)
1. Monarchy--Juvenile literature. 2. Monarchy--History--Juvenile
literature. I. Title.

JC375.M4 2013
321'.6--dc23
                                                    2013006090

Crabtree Publishing Company

www.crabtreebooks.com   1-800-387-7650

Printed in the U.S.A./042013/SX20130306

Published in Canada
Crabtree Publishing
616 Welland Ave.
St. Catharines, Ontario
L2M 5V6

Published in the United States
Crabtree Publishing
PMB 59051
350 Fifth Avenue, 59th Floor
New York, New York 10118

Published in the
United Kingdom
Crabtree Publishing
Maritime House
Basin Road North, Hove
BN41 1WR

Published in Australia
Crabtree Publishing
3 Charles Street
Coburg North
VIC 3058

CONTENTS

THE NEED FOR GOVERNMENT

A government is a group of people and **institutions** that lead and organize a community. Governments of countries create laws, collect taxes, protect a country's borders, and provide people with services. Every country's government works differently, but there are several main types. They include democracy, **dictatorship**, **theocracy**, **oligarchy**, and monarchy.

Akihito, the emperor of Japan since 1989, is believed to be related to the first Japanese emperor. Japan's monarchy is the longest continuous dynasty in history.

What Is a Monarchy?

Monarchy is a form of government in which one person rules for life. The word *monarchy* means "to govern alone." It comes from the Greek words *mono*, meaning "alone," and *archein*, meaning "to rule." The leaders of monarchies are called monarchs.

Monarchs are not usually elected. Most of the time, they inherit their power from an older **generation**. People who live in monarchies generally have great respect for their leaders. Some believe that monarchs received the right to govern directly from God.

Periods of time when a single family is in power are called dynasties. Dynasties can last for hundreds of years.

A Monarch's Power

A monarch's power depends on a country's history and culture. Some monarchs have total power over their governments. In other monarchies, a leader shares power with an elected government. In still other monarchies, monarchs have no power to actually govern. Called figureheads, these monarchs fill only a **ceremonial** role. They participate in important events and serve as a symbol of their country's history.

Throughout history, most governments were monarchies. In fact, almost every country in the world was once ruled by a monarch. Today there are far fewer monarchies than there once were. Some monarchs are quite powerful, but most have only ceremonial roles.

What Is in a Name?

When people think of monarchs, they often think of kings and queens. But monarchs can have other titles too. Just as a king rules a kingdom, an emperor rules an empire. An emperor's wife is called an empress. An empress can also be a woman who is in charge of an empire. Tsars (or czars) are what monarchs of eastern Europe and Russia were called. Monarchs of Muslim states are often called sultans.

The sultan of Oman, who rules his country completely, met the queen of England in 2010. Her role as ruler is primarily ceremonial.

THE BRITISH MONARCHY

Today the best-known monarchy in the world is probably the British monarchy. Since 1952, the leader of the monarchy in the United Kingdom has been Queen Elizabeth II. She is also the monarch for 16 **Commonwealth** nations. These countries were once part of the British Empire.

Rise of an Empire

About 1,200 years ago, the tribes of Britain and Ireland began to unite under leaders. For centuries, different monarchies ruled the kingdoms of England, Wales, Scotland, and Ireland. Over time, the British monarchy joined with the monarchies of Wales, Scotland, and Northern Ireland. Beginning in the 1500s, the British monarchy built an empire around the globe. They created colonies in Jamaica, Australia, Canada, India, and elsewhere. The people in these colonies were **subjects** of the British monarch.

Throughout history, British kings and queens had the power to create and enforce laws. Sometimes monarchs took advice from a group of local leaders. This group slowly evolved into a body of elected lawmakers called Parliament.

The British monarchy owns many palaces and castles. Today they serve as homes, government buildings, and historic monuments. The two best-known royal homes are Buckingham Palace (below) and Windsor Castle.

The Queen (far right) takes part in more than 400 events and ceremonies every year.

Limits on Power

Over time, the British people began to demand a say in how their country was run. They wanted to have rights and democratically elect their leaders. In 1689, England passed a **Bill of Rights**. The Bill of Rights limited the monarch from acting without the approval of Parliament. It also guaranteed certain freedoms to the people.

Today the United Kingdom is governed by Parliament. The leader of Parliament is called a prime minister. The British monarch no longer has the authority to govern. Instead, the British Parliament governs "in the Queen's honor."

The Queen is the United Kingdom's head of state. A country's head of state is the official leader of the government. He or she represents the country to other nations. However, the British monarch's daily duties are ceremonial. The queen hosts ceremonies, appears at public events, and takes part in many charities. Members of the royal family also raise the **morale** of the country in difficult times.

Queen for a Day

Just because Elizabeth II does not govern, that does not mean she is not busy! Every morning, she replies to some of the hundreds of letters she receives daily. She then reviews many government reports. She holds brief meetings with **diplomats**, military leaders, or other honored guests. In the evenings, she may meet with a foreign leader. One evening each week, she meets with the prime minister. The content of those meetings is kept strictly secret.

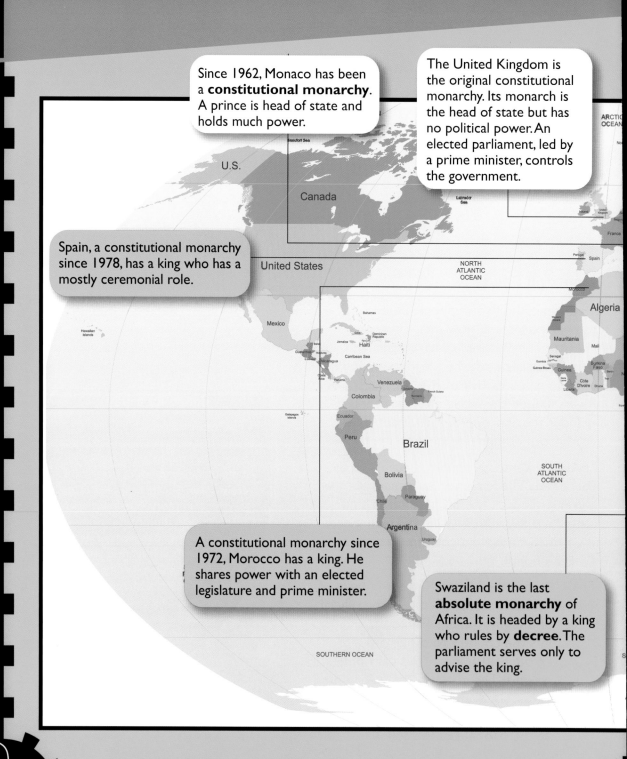

Since 1962, Monaco has been a **constitutional monarchy**. A prince is head of state and holds much power.

The United Kingdom is the original constitutional monarchy. Its monarch is the head of state but has no political power. An elected parliament, led by a prime minister, controls the government.

Spain, a constitutional monarchy since 1978, has a king who has a mostly ceremonial role.

A constitutional monarchy since 1972, Morocco has a king. He shares power with an elected legislature and prime minister.

Swaziland is the last **absolute monarchy** of Africa. It is headed by a king who rules by **decree**. The parliament serves only to advise the king.

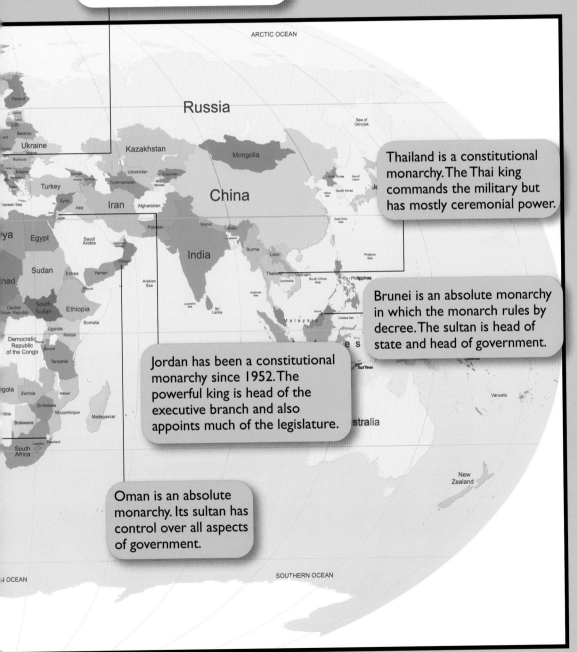

The prince of Liechtenstein, a constitutional monarchy, shares power with its elected legislature. The powerful monarch can dismiss the government.

Thailand is a constitutional monarchy. The Thai king commands the military but has mostly ceremonial power.

Brunei is an absolute monarchy in which the monarch rules by decree. The sultan is head of state and head of government.

Jordan has been a constitutional monarchy since 1952. The powerful king is head of the executive branch and also appoints much of the legislature.

Oman is an absolute monarchy. Its sultan has control over all aspects of government.

THE FIRST MONARCHIES

Many historians believe that some of the earliest governments resembled monarchies. Around 5000 BCE, hunter-gatherers settled into farming communities. They chose the strongest leaders to protect them. These leaders often passed their power down to their **descendants**.

Egyptian and Roman Empires

One of the first civilizations, Egypt had the longest-running monarchy in history. It lasted from 3500 BCE to 30 BCE. During that time, other monarchies emerged in places such as Greece, Rome, Persia, Japan, China, and Vietnam. Like the pharaohs, or kings, of ancient Egypt, many monarchs claimed to be gods or descendants of gods.

A major monarchy ruled the large and powerful Roman Empire in 27 BCE. By its height in around 100 CE, the Roman Empire had expanded to the borders of Portugal, Kuwait, Great Britain, and Sudan.

The Father of Europe

Charlemagne was the leader of a warrior tribe called the Franks in the 700s. Charlemagne's goal was to unite Europe's many small kingdoms. They were to be ruled under one king, one code of law, and one religion—Christianity. By 800, Charlemagne had become king of a large Christian empire across Europe. After his death in 813, his kingdom was divided among his **heirs**. His descendants became the first monarchs of France, Germany, and Italy.

Augustus Caesar was one of the most successful emperors of the Roman Empire. He ruled during a time of great wealth, from 27 BCE to 14 CE.

European Monarch

After the fall of the Roman Empire in about 476 CE, a new era of monarchy began in Europe. It was based on a **class** system called **feudalism**. In this system, poor peasants called serfs farmed plots of land controlled by **lords**. The serfs gave the lords much of their crops and livestock. In exchange, the lords protected the serfs with their soldiers. The king was usually the most wealthy and powerful lord.

Between 1400 and 1750, monarchies reached the height of their power in Europe. Monarchs from Spain, Portugal, Italy, and France sent explorers around the world and established trade routes.

The Benin Empire

During that time, powerful monarchs also existed in Asia, Africa and the Middle East. The Benin Empire was a major monarchy in Africa that existed from the 1300s to 1897. The Benin Empire became wealthy in part by trading with the Europeans. The powerful monarch, called an oba, lived in an extravagant palace in the kingdom's capital, Benin City. By the 1600s, the empire stretched across a major portion of western Africa.

Under the feudal system, knights received land from lords in exchange for military service for the king.

3500 BCE–30 BCE	Pharaohs reigned in ancient Egypt
27 BCE–476 CE	Roman Empire expanded
476–1400	Feudal system dominated Europe
1300s–1897	Benin Empire thrived in Africa

People living in monarchies began to challenge the power of their leaders during the 1600s and the 1700s. This period, called the **Enlightenment**, was a time of great change in science, technology, religion, and **philosophy**. During that time, people became more educated and demanded a greater say in their government.

People revolted against rulers who were **corrupt**. In 1649, the British people overthrew and beheaded King Charles I. By 1689, the British people had created a constitution to limit the power of the monarch. American colonists broke away from Britain in 1776 and signed the Declaration of Independence. In 1789, the people of France revolted against Louis XVI. Soon after, the French people ended their country's monarchy.

Loss of Power

Monarchs continued to lose power during the 1800s and 1900s. People living under strong monarchies demanded that they become weaker. Citizens of some countries overthrew their monarchies completely. The last monarch of Germany, Kaiser Wilhelm II, gave up his throne after his country's terrible loss in World War I (1914–1918). The last Russian monarch, Tsar Nicholas II, was overthrown in 1918 by a group called the **Bolsheviks**. The Bolsheviks established a new kind of government called **communism**.

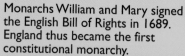

Monarchs William and Mary signed the English Bill of Rights in 1689. England thus became the first constitutional monarchy.

Many more monarchies ended after **World War II** (1939–1945). Japan lost that war to the **Allies**, including the United States. After the war, the Allies established a new constitution for Japan. It stripped the monarchy of most of its power. After the war, the United Kingdom no longer had the resources to run its vast empire. Many of its colonies gained their independence. People who had long been part of the British monarchy were free to create their own governments.

By the 2000s, few powerful monarchs remained. Most monarchs either share power with democratically elected leaders or act as figureheads for their country.

Changes in government can lead to violence. When Russia descended into civil war at the end of World War I, Tsar Nicholas II and his family were executed.

Monarchy in China

For 2,000 years, powerful emperors ruled China. During the Han, Sui, Tang, and Song dynasties (202 BCE–1279 CE), China's size and population expanded. Arts, literature, and science flourished. The Chinese people overthrew China's last dynasty, the Qing Dynasty, in 1912. In 1949, a communist government took over rule of China.

1649	King Charles I of England overthrown
1689	England passed Bill of Rights
1776	American colonies declared independence from England
1789	French monarchy is overthrown
1912	Puyi, last monarch of China, is overthrown
1918	Last German monarch, Kaiser Wilhelm II, gives up throne
1918	Last Russian monarch, Tsar Nicholas II, is overthrown

TYPES OF MONARCHIES

There are many kinds of monarchies. The leaders of some monarchies have control over all parts of government. Other monarchs share power with elected governments. The two main types are called absolute monarchies and constitutional monarchies. Absolute monarchies were the most common form of government for centuries.

King Louis XIV, who ruled France from 1643 to 1715, was an absolute monarch. He once declared, "*L'état, c'est moi.*" The statement means "I am the state."

Absolute Monarchy

In absolute monarchies, the rulers hold absolute, or total, power. These monarchs can raise and collect taxes, declare wars, create their own laws, and jail and kill their enemies. Many people believed that absolute monarchs received the right to govern directly from God. In Europe, this belief was called the Divine Right of Kings. In China and eastern Asia, a similar idea was known as the Mandate from Heaven.

Today many absolute monarchies are corrupt. Laws limit their power, but the monarchs regularly break them. In 1968, Swaziland, the last absolute monarchy of Africa, passed a constitution to create a democratic government. Five years later, however, the Swazi king suspended the constitution. He claimed it was unpopular with the people.

Means to an End?

The Italian Niccolo Machiavelli believed in absolute monarchy. He wrote *The Prince* in 1513. He argued that an absolute ruler was the only sure way for any society to be peaceful and wealthy. He also thought rulers could use any means to keep power, no matter how ruthless. Many absolute rulers have used *The Prince* to defend cruel decisions.

Constitutional Monarchy

In a constitutional or limited monarchy, a constitution limits a monarch's power. A constitution is a written summary of the country's important laws and rights. There are several different kinds of constitutional monarchies.

In some constitutional monarchies, leaders have the power to create and enforce laws. For instance, in Monaco, the monarch and the elected legislature share power. However, the monarch is responsible for proposing all the country's laws. The parliament meets only a few times a year to vote on these laws.

Leaders of other constitutional monarchies have little or no power to govern. These monarchs have mainly ceremonial roles. They participate in their country's traditions and important events. Most European monarchs hold ceremonial positions only.

In many constitutional monarchies such as Canada's, members of elected legislatures write the country's laws.

CHANGING MONARCHIES

Today many people living in absolute monarchies are demanding a greater say in their government. Absolute monarchs also face pressure from other countries to give their people more rights. At the same time, however, some people believe a strong monarchy is necessary. For these reasons, monarchies around the world are changing. In many countries, those changes have been rocky.

Disagreement over the role of the monarch and corruption in the government has led to protests in Thailand. Many Thai people support the royal family.

Thailand's Turmoil

In Thailand, the monarch was once powerful. Today his role is mainly ceremonial. The current monarch, King Bhumibol Adulyadej, has been in power since 1950. During that time, Thailand has struggled to set up a democracy. There have been 15 military **coups**, 27 prime ministers, and at least nine constitutions. In 2006, the government was seized by a group of military members called a **junta**. In 2007, the governing junta passed a new constitution. It set up a new democratic government with a constitutional monarchy. The Thai people continue to protest those changes today.

Juntas

In some cases, military leaders have formed revolutionary groups, called juntas, to overthrow a monarch. Though monarchs often have great power, without the support of their people and other members of government, the monarch's position—and life—could be in danger.

Limited Monarchy in Morocco

The role of Morocco's monarch has been changing for decades. According to the country's laws, the king shares power with the elected parliament. In the past, the king has had much more power than the elected government. But the king has lost power over the years. Morocco passed new constitutions in 1962, 1972, 1992, 1996, and 2011. Each of these constitutions placed greater limits on the king's power. Each has also given more power to the elected parliament and prime minister. For example, the king used to appoint diplomats and ambassadors. Now those appointments are a responsibility of the prime minister.

Power to the Prince

In contrast, the people in the tiny country of Liechtenstein have voted several times to give its monarch greater power. Liechtenstein is a constitutional monarchy with a 25-person legislature. The prince has had enormous authority for a long time. For example, he could reject any law passed by the legislature. In 2004, the people voted to give him the power to fire entire governments. In July 2012, the people of Liechtenstein rejected another proposal to limit the prince's power.

Liechtenstein's parliament has little power.

RIGHTS OF THE PEOPLE

In a monarchy, the rights of the people depend on many factors. People are more likely to have rights if there is a constitution in place. A fair and just ruler is also more likely to give his people rights than a corrupt ruler.

No Guarantees

In an absolute monarchy, people have no guaranteed rights at all. The monarch is all-powerful. An absolute monarch can decide to give some people more privileges than others. These privileges are not rights, however. An absolute ruler can take them away at any moment.

Some absolute monarchies distribute rights unequally, according to the country's culture or religion. The kingdom of Swaziland, for instance, is known for **violating** human rights. One example is the country's treatment of women. The country's laws guarantee women equal treatment. However, in daily life, women have few rights and are treated differently than men. They are not allowed to own property or open bank accounts without a man's permission. They can even be fined for wearing pants.

In Swaziland, Queen Mother Ntombi (right) is considered the spiritual head of state. Her title is the Indlovukazi, or Great She Elephant, of Swaziland. King Mswati III (left) of Swaziland is her son.

Constitutional Rights

In constitutional monarchies, the rights of the people are written in a constitution. Different countries have different constitutions. However, most protect rights such as freedom of speech, freedom from cruel and unusual punishment, and the right to a fair trial. In many constitutional monarchies, these rights are enforced. In other monarchies, such as absolute monarchies, leaders only claim to protect the rights of their people. Instead they violate these rights if it benefits them.

In many countries, monarchies do not allow free speech. Criticizing the monarchy is illegal in absolute monarchies and constitutional monarchies. In 2011, a Thai man was sentenced to 20 years in prison for sending personal text messages that criticized the Thai king.

Enlightenment thinker Jean-Jacques Rousseau promoted the idea of individual rights.

A Bright Idea

It seems strange now but, for hundreds of years, people didn't believe in individual rights. In the 1600s and 1700s, people began to question the power of monarchs and argue for more individual rights. This period of time was called the Enlightenment. English philosopher John Locke believed that people were born with certain rights. Jean-Jacques Rousseau, a French writer, argued that the purpose of government was to protect the rights of people. Enlightenment ideas led directly to the French and American Revolutions. They also influenced new governments for centuries afterward.

People living in monarchies play different roles in their government. Their responsibilities depend on what kind of monarchy they live in.

Seen and Not Heard

In absolute monarchies, people usually play a small part in government. The monarch makes most of the decisions in the government. The monarch appoints leaders and sets the country's policies. In addition, people in absolute monarchies often do not have the freedom to criticize their government.

The main way people participate in absolute monarchies is by supporting the monarch and obeying the laws. It may be surprising that most monarchs, even absolute monarchs, are supported and respected by the majority of their people.

For example, Brunei is an absolute monarchy. It has held only one election in the past 60 years, in 1963. During that time, the sultan, Hassanal Bolkiah, has made all the decisions for the country. He also appointed his advisors and the country's judges. In 2004, the sultan announced that he would reform parliament. However, he has not scheduled any elections.

A Louder Voice

In constitutional monarchies, citizens usually play a larger part in their government than in absolute monarchies. In many constitutional monarchies, people vote to elect many or all of the people who create laws and run the government.

For example, in the United Kingdom, the people elect members of Parliament at regular intervals. Members of government can ask for advice from the monarch, but the monarch has no authority to govern. People participate in government by voting for the leaders they support.

People living in monarchies show their support for the monarch by attending events and ceremonies. In 2008, King Mswati III celebrated the 40th year of Swaziland's independence.

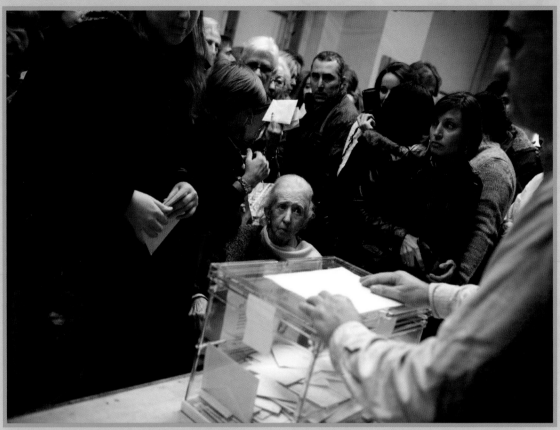

One way people participate in constitutional monarchies is by voting for members of government. The people do not elect the monarch, however.

In other constitutional monarchies, the laws make it more difficult for people to participate. In Morocco, the monarch held great power over the elected legislators. Before a 2011 constitutional reform, the king had to approve every bill passed by the elected legislature before it could become law.

People in constitutional monarchies also participate by sharing their opinions about issues. Freedom of speech is a right that is guaranteed in the constitutions of many countries. However, even in constitutional monarchies, people are often not permitted to criticize the monarchy.

Rule by Decree

It is often said that absolute monarchs rule by decree. A decree is an order issued by a head of state that has the force of law. Unlike other laws, it does not need to be approved by a legislature or any other body.

ROYAL BLOOD

Bloodlines of absolute monarchs have long been considered holy. This view allows power to be passed down through family members. The longest unbroken royal bloodline in history is Japan's monarchy.

Order of Succession

Different countries, empires, and kingdoms have created different rules for **hereditary succession**. A system to decide who inherits power in a monarchy is called the order of succession. Throughout much of history, royal titles were passed down to the firstborn son.

Women have also inherited the throne in some cases. In many monarchies, women can become leaders only if they are the sole direct descendants of the monarch. If there is no direct descendant, power is usually passed to other relatives according to the country's system.

Only six monarchies in Europe have given men and women an equal chance to inherit the throne. Sweden became the first European monarchy to do so in 1980. It was followed by Norway, the Netherlands, Belgium, Denmark, and Luxembourg. In 2011, the Commonwealth countries of Great Britain voted to eliminate the male preference in the United Kingdom's monarchy.

The United Kingdom is expected to pass a law that would allow the first child of Prince William and Kate Middleton, boy or girl, to become the monarch.

King Juan Carlos (right) interviews members of parliament before appointing the president. Mariano Rajoy (left) was made Spain's president in 2011. In many other monarchies, the head of government is chosen by the parliament.

Advisors and Lawmakers

Although monarchs inherit their positions in constitutional monarchies, other leaders are selected in other ways. In many constitutional monarchies, such as Thailand and Monaco, all of the members of the legislatures are elected. In other monarchies, the monarch appoints a portion of the legislature. The country's citizens elect the other portion. In some absolute monarchies, the ruler appoints all the advisors and legislators.

The monarch often appoints the leader of government, such as the prime minister, from members of the elected legislature. This is the case in both Spain and Morocco. In other monarchies, the members of the legislature vote to decide the head of government.

Elective Monarchies

Historians think that leaders of some of the earliest monarchies were chosen through elections. Most elective monarchies did not last. Elections were difficult in large empires because of the amount of territory they covered. Plus leaders did not want to give up power. Most elective monarchies changed into hereditary monarchies. However, forms of elective monarchies still exist in Malaysia and Cambodia.

In Charge

In absolute monarchies, the monarch has the final say in any decision. Absolute monarchs may appoint advisory councils, diplomats, and other assistants to help them make decisions. However, final choices always rest with the single ruler. In some cases, a monarch inherits a crown but is too young to rule. Then an advisor, called a regent, governs until the heir becomes old enough to rule.

Limited Power

In many constitutional monarchies, monarchs have executive power. They run the government and put the laws to work. They may have the power to command the military. An elected body has legislative power. It makes the laws.

Leaders have different degrees of power, depending on their constitutions. Most monarchs represent their countries in meetings with foreign leaders. Many also approve legislators and appoint ministers, advisors, and judges.

The sultan of Brunei is also its prime minister, minister of defense and finance, and supreme commander of the military.

Though she has no power to govern, Queen Elizabeth II receives daily updates about the events in Parliament. She must sign every law Parliament passes.

Some monarchs with executive power can cancel laws the legislature has approved. They can even shut down the legislature.

In constitutional monarchies with ceremonial monarchs, monarchs have little or no executive power. Elected leaders meet with foreign leaders, appoint ministers, and command the military. Still, ceremonial monarchs often take part in many symbolic activities.

Loss of Power in Japan

From 1926 until 1989, Emperor Hirohito ruled Japan. Like previous Japanese emperors, Hirohito was believed to have been chosen by God. He became an absolute ruler, refusing to share power with the country's elected legislature. He also expanded Japan's empire using military force. Japan joined Germany in World War II and fought against the Allies. After Japan's defeat, the Allies helped Japan draft a new constitution to establish a democratic government. The new constitution took away the emperor's absolute rule and his claim to a divine right. Today, Japan's emperor has no power to govern. His role is merely ceremonial.

Possible heirs to the throne have always had a reason to compete for power. After all, the sooner the monarch dies, the sooner the heir gains power. Killing a monarch for any reason is called regicide.

In Swaziland, the king's wives compete to be the one to give birth to the heir. The Swazi king marries a woman from each of the country's provinces. The wife who bears him a son first becomes the queen mother, the spiritual head of state.

Positions in the Monarchy

Monarchies have access to great wealth and power. In fact, absolute monarchies control all of their country's money. In some monarchies, rulers appoint the leaders of government-owned businesses.

People compete for positions in the government for the chance to possibly share in the monarch's riches and power. This is especially true in poor countries where people have few opportunities to earn a living. Getting a position working for the royal family could be the only chance for a wealthy future.

Regicide

Throughout history, many monarchs have been murdered by their family. In 1975 in Saudi Arabia, Prince Faysal ibn Musad murdered his uncle, King Faysal. The king's half brother, Crown Prince Khalid then took the throne.

The current Swazi king, Mswati III, has 14 wives and 23 children.

In 2011, peaceful demonstrators in Morocco protested. They wanted greater changes to the constitution and social justice.

People Power

Some absolute monarchies are changing to constitutional monarchies with a democratic government. In these countries, the monarch competes for power with the people.

In Morocco, thousands of protests called for more democracy and a weaker monarchy in 2011. As a result, the king formed a group to study the constitution. It made several changes to the constitution. They made the elected prime minister the head of government, not the monarch. Many Moroccans still want an even weaker king.

In constitutional monarchies where elected leaders run the government, political parties, interest groups, and corporations compete for power. In Spain, there are many political parties, but two main political parties have the most members in parliament. They are the People's Party and the Spanish Socialist Workers' Party.

LOCAL GOVERNMENTS

A country's national government handles the issues and passes laws that affect the entire country. Most countries are also divided into smaller regions or provinces. The governments of these regions deal with local issues, such as collecting garbage and enforcing laws locally.

Selection of Local Rulers

In absolute monarchies, local rulers run the provinces on behalf of the monarch. Local rulers are often members of the royal family or members of respected families. Saudi Arabia, for instance, is divided into 13 provinces. Each province is headed by a mayor who is chosen by the king. The Saudi mayors do not make independent decisions. Their job is to carry out the king's policies.

In constitutional monarchies, local leaders can be selected in different ways. In some constitutional monarchies, the monarch appoints local leaders. Morocco is divided into 61 regions. Each region is run by a leader, and that leader is appointed by the Moroccan king. In other constitutional monarchies, members of an elected government appoint local or regional leaders.

In still other constitutional monarchies, local rulers are democratically elected. This is the case in Spain. Spain is made up of 17 communities that elect their own leaders. These local governments have great freedom to govern themselves. They follow rules outlined in the constitution.

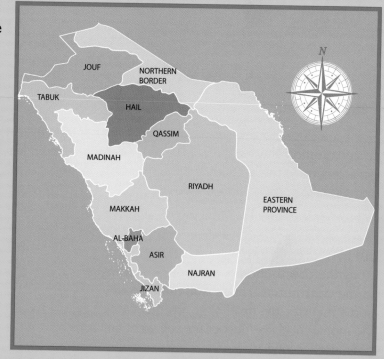

Sometimes the mayors of provinces in Saudi Arabia are members of the royal Saudi family.

Many of Brunei's villages are quite poor. The leader of the national government, the sultan, is one of the richest people in the world.

Small Monarchies

Several monarchies are so small that they do not have local rulers. Liechtenstein, for example, is only 62.5 square miles (162 square km). That is the size of Washington, D.C. The people of Liechtenstein are represented by 25 elected members of the national legislature.

Brunei is another small country that does not have formal local governments. However, villagers do traditionally select local leaders. These leaders are responsible for looking after the people in their communities.

Government in the Ottoman Empire

Today many monarchies guarantee religious freedom. However, throughout history, some monarchies executed their citizens for following a religion that differed from the state religion. The Ottoman Empire (1299–1918) once stretched across the Middle East, southeastern Europe, and North Africa. It was a Muslim empire, but it allowed its religious minorities unusual freedoms. Ottoman emperors gave minorities the right to manage their local governments. This practice became known as the millet system. The millet system helped the Ottoman Empire expand, because minorities had less reason to resist joining the empire.

ORIGIN OF LAWS

For a society to function, there must be laws. Different monarchies base their laws on different sources. Many monarchies base their laws on civil law, a written legal system that began in Rome and western Europe in the 500s CE. Legal systems can also be based on common laws. These unwritten laws come from a country's traditions and history. Many monarchies use a combination of civil law and common law.

Court System

In most modern monarchies, the judicial branch is separate from the legislature and the monarch. In some monarchies, the monarch appoints the judges. In others, that decision is up to an elected head of government, such as a prime minister.

In some absolute monarchies, the courts are separate. However, the monarch often has the right to **intervene**.

Religious Law

Throughout history, monarchies have also often based their legal systems on religious law. This was true for European monarchies during the Middle Ages from about 500 to 1500 CE. During that time, Christian churches ran many legal courts. These courts based their laws on religious guidelines outlined in the Bible or accepted by Church leaders.

Today, many Islamic monarchies base their laws on Islamic law, also called Sharia law. Muslim rulers developed Sharia law during the 700s and 800s. It is based on two sources, the Quran, the Muslim holy book, and the Sunna, the examples set by the Islamic prophet Muhammad. Sharia law describes different crimes and lists how each should be punished. It also tells Muslims how they should live.

Islamic law is not the same in every Muslim country. Not all Muslims agree on the meaning of the rules contained in the Quran and the Sunna.

The judicial branch of constitutional monarchies interprets the laws of the nation.

Passing Laws

In absolute monarchies such as Oman and Saudi Arabia, the monarch does not need to pass laws. The monarch rules by decree, which means any monarch's order is a law.

A constitutional monarch's role in creating laws is outlined in a country's constitution. The constitution also contains the country's most important laws. Any new laws created should not go against the constitution.

In constitutional monarchies, legislatures typically pass laws. In many monarchies, the monarch officially signs all legislation but has no power to reject it. In other constitutional monarchies, monarchs do have the power to reject laws passed by the legislature. Some constitutional monarchs have fired entire legislatures because they did not pass certain laws.

Treason

One of the most serious crimes in a monarchy has always been treason, or disloyalty to the crown. In many monarchies, criticizing the monarch is still a crime. Treason also includes more serious acts, such as plotting to murder the monarch or supporting the monarch's enemies. In some monarchies, these crimes can be punishable by death.

CONTROLLING THE WEALTH

In absolute monarchies, all of the country's wealth belongs to the monarch and the royal family. Absolute monarchs can invest that wealth as they wish and profit from private industry in their countries. Throughout much of history, monarchs funded artists, musicians, and industries. Monarchs often distributed the empire's land and wealth to lords to manage.

Monarchies Make Money

Beginning in the 1400s, the monarchs of Europe began funding explorers' expeditions to find new oversea trade routes. In 1492, Spain's Queen Isabella I sent Christopher Columbus to find a route to India. Instead, he landed on an island off what is now the Florida coast. Over the next several decades, other explorers from Spain, Portugal, England, and France discovered new sea routes. They set up trading posts around the world. The new trade routes and trading posts made the European monarchies even richer and helped start new businesses.

Today, monarchs use their wealth to invest in different companies and projects. In Morocco, the government controls several companies. Until recently, the king had the power to appoint the companies' management. The king of Thailand is the richest monarch in the world. He invests money in different industries from a fund called the Crown Property Bureau. Thailand's king also funds scholarships, health clinics, and other community projects.

Natural resources contribute greatly to the wealth of monarchies. For instance, oil is plentiful in the Middle East. This resource has made the monarchs and royal families in that region some of the richest people in the world. These countries include Saudi Arabia, Oman, and Qatar. Brunei has also become a very rich monarchy because of the oil found in Southeast Asia.

Rulers of monarchies are very wealthy. During the 1600s, Emperor Shah Jahan of India used his wealth to build the Taj Mahal. This palace honors his dead wife.

Hands Off

Constitutional monarchs who have ceremonial roles generally have no official power over their countries' economy or trade policies. That power is given to an elected government. Governments often appoint a minister or cabinet member to influence private businesses or create laws to regulate them.

However, even monarchs who have no official power over the economy can still influence the financial situations of their countries. They can do this by giving advice to the government or helping them to negotiate with other countries. Spain's King, Juan Carlos, is known for giving advice to his government about economic matters.

There is typically an enormous contrast between the lifestyle of the royal family and the lifestyle of the average citizen.

Monarchs' Money

Monarchies are funded by a mix of taxes and the monarchs' own money. Monarchs typically use some of the private wealth and property they have inherited. This wealth is invested in various funds that produce income. Monarchs and royal families also receive a specific amount of money raised from taxes. In most cases, the government gives a constitutional monarchy a certain amount of money.

MONARCHS AND THE MEDIA

Though they have little or no power to govern, today's constitutional monarchs play an important role in their countries. Some of their most important roles involve the media, such as the Internet, television, newspapers, magazines, and radio.

Sending a Message

One of the roles of many monarchs is to encourage national pride. They mark important events in history with speeches and grand ceremonies. Since the invention of mass communication in the 1900s, monarchs' words reach people quickly and directly. Such speeches can serve to inspire people in times of crisis.

Covering Events

Members of the royal family also make appearances to bring attention to community events. They appear at art galleries, homeless shelters, factories, and schools. They also take part in many charities and publicly support international causes.

Queen Rania of Jordan, for example, focuses on improving primary education in Jordan and around the world. The monarch's presence at these events helps bring national attention from the media.

The United Kingdom's King George VI stuttered. He faced the challenging task of using the radio to speak to his people on the eve of World War II. He delivered a strong, heartfelt message to help his country prepare for battle.

The press flock to photograph royal marriages. The prince of Luxembourg will inherit his country's throne.

Free Press and Censorship

The government does not control a free press. Reporters are allowed to express any opinion they want. In countries with a free press, the media may criticize the monarchy. In the United Kingdom and other European countries, people often debate whether the monarchy should still exist.

In other monarchies, leaders have tried to control the media. The government of Oman, for instance, **censors** the Internet and other media. It keeps out material that criticizes the government, the royal family, and other topics that concern the monarchy. The nearby monarchies of Saudi Arabia and Qatar do the same.

Monarch Mania

Members of royal families are some of the world's biggest celebrities. Magazines and newspapers examine their personal lives, hoping to uncover a scandal. This obsession is not new. People have gossiped about royal families for hundreds of years. Because of their global fame, the British monarchy may face the most media attention. Prince William's mother, Princess Diana, was stalked by journalists for much of her public life. In August 1997, she died in a car crash while trying to escape from the **paparazzi**.

CULTURAL INFLUENCE

Culture is the arts, achievements, beliefs, customs, and ideas that have developed in a community over time. Throughout history, monarchs influenced their countries' culture in a variety of ways.

Art Collectors

Monarchs once used their wealth to fund artists, musicians, architects, and writers. Live music and theater was regularly performed at the royal household, called the court. Paintings, symphonies, and plays funded by the monarch became popular and influential.

Monarchs continue to play a role in the arts. Royal families often host cultural events at the royal homes. They also preserve large collections of art, furniture, and jewels that have been passed down through generations. The collections contain a lot of information about a country's culture and history.

Royal families own homes, pieces of art, and other objects that date back hundreds of years.

Elizabethan England

Queen Elizabeth I, who ruled England from 1533 to 1603, was a great **patron** of the arts. She regularly funded symphonies and plays. During her reign, nobles throughout England did the same. As a result, the later years of her rule, called the Elizabethan Age, produced many celebrated works of literature. Writers such as playwright and poet William Shakespeare are still read today. Theater became popular under Elizabeth I. People from all classes attended public theaters.

The laws created by absolute rulers can have effects on culture. Laws limit the freedom of women in Saudi Arabia. Women cannot drive and must wear veils. These laws create a culture dominated by the ideas of men.

Model Culture

Monarchs have also affected their country's culture by setting examples. The fashions worn by the royal family have often influenced their subjects' style. For example, Marie Antoinette was the queen of France from 1755 to 1793. She set the style for her subjects, rich and poor alike. They tried to copy her fashion choices, from her ankle-length dresses to her 3-foot (1-m) tower of powdered hair.

Today, monarchs and members of royal families are as famous as other celebrities. The fashion choices of famous royals greatly affect the tastes of their citizens. Thanks to the photographers who publish their photos in magazines and on the Internet, they can be seen by people around the world.

Culture Connection

Finally, monarchies connect people to their country's cultural history. The ceremonies they participate in have often existed for hundreds of years. For example, the ritual performed to crown a new British monarch has changed very little in 1,000 years.

The speeches monarchs give and events they take part in are also reminders of their country's cultural history. Many people see a link to history as one of the most important responsibilities of monarchies today.

FORMS OF GOVERNMENT

	Democracy	Dictatorship
Basis of power	People elect officials to represent their views and beliefs.	The dictator controls everything in the country. His word is the law.
Rights of the people	People have many rights, including the right to fair and free elections, the right to assemble, and the right to choose how to live their lives.	The people have very few rights. Their duty is to do whatever the dictator wants.
How leaders are chosen	Frequent and regular elections are held to vote for leaders.	Leaders can inherit their position or take it with military force. The most powerful political party may also choose them.
Basis of judicial branch	A separate judicial branch enforces the laws made by the legislative branch. Laws are supposed to be enforced freely and fairly.	The judicial branch does what the dictator wants.
Relation of business to the form of government	Government plays a limited role in businesses. They may charge taxes and make some laws to make sure businesses are run fairly.	The government often owns the major businesses in a country.
Control of media	The government does not control the media. People have access to many opinions and diverse information from the media.	The dictator either tells the media what to report or censors the media's reports.
Role of religion	People may choose to practice their own religion.	People may or may not be able to practice their religion freely. However, political parties and focus on the dictator's personality are more important than religion.

Monarchy	Oligarchy	Theocracy
A monarch's power is inherited from a previous generation. In absolute monarchies, monarchs are believed to be chosen by God.	A select few use their wealth or secret connections to powerful people in the government to control the country. They are rarely elected.	The government is based on the state religion.
Rights are not guaranteed in an absolute monarchy. In a constitutional monarchy, rights are outlined in the country's constitution.	No rights are guaranteed, but in elected oligarchies, citizens can vote.	The laws of the state religion limit the rights of the people.
Power is passed down through families. Monarchies have different rules for who inherits power. In constitutional monarchies, the leaders of governing bodies, such as a parliament, are chosen through elections.	Oligarchs take power in most cases. They are rarely elected. They usually lead hidden behind the government.	Leaders are elected, appointed, or chosen by religious customs.
In absolute monarchies, monarchs run the courts. Most constitutional monarchies have a separate judicial branch to ensure fair treatment.	Most oligarchies hide behind regular government functions. With their money and power, they affect the judicial branch's decisions.	All laws are based on the state religion. The judicial branch bases its judgments on that religion's laws.
Leaders of absolute monarchies control all of the wealth of a country. In constitutional monarchies, decisions about business are made by a governing body, such as a parliament.	Many oligarchs control wealthy businesses.	Businesses can be owned by citizens or by the government.
The press is not free in an absolute monarchy. Many constitutional monarchies, however, guarantee freedom of the media and speech.	Oligarchs tend to own and control all the media.	The media can be controlled by the government or by private citizens. It must follow the laws of the state religion.
Absolute monarchies often require people to have the same religion as the monarch. Many constitutional monarchies guarantee freedom of religion.	Some oligarchs share a common religion.	Religion forms the basis of the government. It dictates most aspects of the citizens' lives.

There are several advantages of successful monarchies. Monarchs typically come from wealthy families and are well educated. Because they inherit their positions, monarchs are trained from birth to understand their responsibilities. In other forms of government, elected leaders are less likely to be so well prepared and trained.

Other Advantages

Monarchs give countries some stability because they are in power for life. In democracies, leaders have term limits. Every few years, new leaders are elected. Completely new policies may be put in place. In contrast, monarchs can rule for several decades. When monarchs share power with an elected government, they can provide a source of wisdom.

Finally, monarchies remind their citizens of the country's history and traditions. Monarchs are often related to rulers who held office hundreds of years ago. They also participate in ceremonies that are hundreds of years old, giving the country a sense of national pride.

As of 2013, King Bhumibol Adulyadej of Thailand is the longest-reigning monarch in the world. He has been in power since 1946.

Disadvantages of Monarchies

There are also many disadvantages of monarchies, especially monarchies in which rulers have significant power. People living in these monarchies do not always have rights. Even if a country has a constitution, a powerful ruler can often take away people's rights. Speech is also often limited in monarchies. Even in countries where constitutions guarantee many freedoms, laws restrict people's ability to criticize the ruler.

Citizens of a monarchy also cannot participate in government in the same way people can in a democracy. People cannot elect the monarch, who is often the head of state and sometimes the head of government. If the country is unhappy with the monarch, there is no way to vote him or her out of office.

Finally, in many constitutional monarchies, a monarch is merely a ceremonial figure. In these cases, the monarch is not needed to govern the country. Some people see their position as a waste of time, taxpayers' money, and other resources.

Protesters object to the British monarchy as outdated and a costly use of government funds.

Why Have Constitutional Monarchy?

A constitutional monarchy may seem a logical **compromise** between an absolute monarchy and no monarchy at all. But there are many people today who ask, if the monarchy has little or no power to run the country, why have it at all? In 2007, protests against the king broke out in Spain. Protesters called for the monarchy to give up all power. King Juan Carlos argued that the monarchy has helped the country have a thriving and stable democracy since 1975.

Other British citizens see the monarchy and the royal wedding in 2012 as symbols of national unity.

For hundreds of years, absolute monarchy was a sensible choice for many societies. Monarchies offered poor, struggling populations protection, stability, and leadership. They provided a source of authority and a way to organize society. People believed monarchs were superior to the rest of the population. They respected their rulers, even if their policies were unfair.

Changes Lead to Revolt

Over time, absolute monarchies became less effective forms of government. Scientific discoveries helped people better understand the world. Thanks to the invention of the printing press in 1450, ordinary people could read the ideas of great thinkers. People became more educated and independent. They no longer wanted a ruler to tell them how to live. As a result, people revolted against absolute monarchs. They established new governments to better serve the people.

Many monarchies have shifted between a powerful monarch and more limited one. That process can be rocky. It continues today in countries around the world.

Egypt's first kings, the pharaohs, organized their people into work groups to build huge monuments to honor them. Now Egypt's people are organizing to reduce the power of their king.

Sweden's King Carl XVI Gustaf is the country's head of state, but he has no political power.

Monarchies Today

Like those of the past, today's absolute monarchies exist in countries with huge, unfair differences among the people. A poor, uneducated population allows monarchs to have great power over the lives of their subjects. In fact, it is in the interest of absolute rulers for their population to stay poor and uninformed. Many absolute monarchs try to control the media and keep information from their people.

Many of the challenges monarchies face have been the same for centuries. For example, absolute monarchs must govern effectively for their citizens. They must work to keep the respect of their people. In a time of few absolute monarchs, they must justify why they alone have enormous power.

The challenges of monarchies are more difficult today than ever before. Their subjects are more educated than in the past. Television and the Internet give people access to others' opinions and lifestyles. The media helps people living under **oppressive** governments understand the freedoms people enjoy in other countries.

If absolute monarchs are not respected, their subjects may organize and demand a new form of government. This process is taking place in countries around the world, from Jordan to Morocco to Thailand. Protesters are demanding more rights and a government that allows its people to participate. As the world continues to change, the most successful and stable monarchies will likely be those that are the most democratic.

Niccolo Machiavelli's *The Prince*, published in 1532, contained advice for monarchs. Unlike other writers, he did not promote a monarch doing what was best for his people. He advised doing what was best to stay in power.

Concerning Cruelty and **Clemency**, and Whether It Is Better to Be Loved Than Feared

Upon this a question arises: whether it is better to be loved than feared or feared than loved? It may be answered that one should wish to be both, but, because it is difficult to unite them in one person, it is much safer to be feared than loved, when, of the two, either must be dispensed with. Because this is to be asserted in general of men, that they are ungrateful, fickle, false, cowardly, **covetous**, and as long as you succeed they are yours entirely; they will offer you their blood, property, life, and children, as is said above, when the need is far distant; but when it approaches they turn against you. . . . men have less **scruple** in offending one who is beloved than one who is feared, for love is preserved by the link of obligation which, owing to the baseness of men, is broken at every opportunity for their advantage; but fear preserves you by a dread of punishment which never fails.

Nevertheless a prince ought to inspire fear in such a way that, if he does not win love, he avoids hatred; because he can endure very well being feared whilst he is not hated, which will always be as long as he abstains from the property of his citizens and subjects and from their women.

NICCOLÒ MACCHIAVELLI

Machiavelli thought that a leader who seized a country could control it better than a monarch who inherited power.

English Bill of Rights

The British Parliament passed the Bill of Rights in 1689. One of its basic purposes was to limit the power of the British monarch. However, it also set out certain rights for British citizens. The bill declared the following:

That the pretended power of suspending the laws or the execution of laws by regal authority without consent of Parliament is illegal; ...

That it is the right of the subjects to petition the king, and all commitments and prosecutions for such petitioning are illegal;

That the raising or keeping a standing army within the kingdom in time of peace, unless it be with consent of Parliament, is against law;

That election of members of Parliament ought to be free;

That the freedom of speech and debates or proceedings in Parliament ought not to be impeached or questioned in any court or place out of Parliament ; ...

The British Parliament discussed proposed laws, including the Bill of Rights, and held trials.

GLOSSARY

absolute monarchy A government in which a ruler controls every aspect of government. Rule is passed along family lines.

Allies A group of nations, including the United States, the United Kingdom, Russia, and China, that fought the Axis Powers, including Germany, Italy, and Japan, from 1939 to 1945

Bill of Rights A list of privileges that everyone should have

bloodlines Particular orders of direct lines of ancestors; the lines of descent of a family

Bolsheviks Members of the communist party that seized power in Russia in 1917

censors Prevents publication or deletes ideas thought to be objectionable or that go against the government's views and goals

ceremonial Relating to or used for formal acts or special occasions

class A group or rank of society. Lower classes typically have less money than upper classes.

clemency A tendency to show mercy

Commonwealth An international association consisting of the United Kingdom and countries that were once part of the British Empire

communism A system of government in which a single party controls all businesses and agriculture. Under communism, all property is supposed to be publicly owned, and people work and are paid according to their abilities.

compromise A settlement of an argument by each group giving up some demands

constitutional monarchy A system of government in which a king, queen, or sultan shares power, usually with an elected government. The monarch may be the head of state or a purely ceremonial leader.

corrupt Willing to be dishonest in exchange for money or personal gain

covetous Showing great desire to have something, usually that belongs to someone else

coups Sudden overthrows of the government

decree An order that is issued by a head of state and has the same impact as a law

descendants People who come from a particular ancestor or group of ancestors

dictatorship A government by a person who holds complete authority

diplomats People whose job is to handle the relations between their country and other nations

Enlightenment A time that began during the 1600s in Europe and spread to other countries. Enlightenment thinkers objected to the absolute rule of monarchies.

feudalism A political system during the Middle Ages in western Europe. Under feudalism, a lord provided land and protection for people under his rule and, in return, they promised service and loyalty to the lord.

generation Individuals who are one step in the line of descent of a family. A grandmother, mother, and daughter are three generations of a family.

heirs People who have the right to the title, money, or property of a person who died

hereditary succession A system that explains which relative should take power when a monarch has died

institutions Organizations that are set up for specific reasons

intervene Come between two or more individuals or groups to stop, settle, or change something

junta A group of people controlling a government, especially after a revolution

lords Powerful men in the Middle Ages who lived in manors or castles and had many people under their control

morale The confidence and enthusiasm a person or group feels about what is going on

oligarchy A government in which a small group exercises control. Wealth and power is concentrated in just a few people's hands.

oppressive Describes control or rule by cruel or unfair means

paparazzi Photographers who chase after celebrities for photos

patron A person who supports a group or individual with money or power

philosophy The study of the basic nature and purpose of life, the universe, and truth

scruple A feeling of doubt about whether something is the right thing to do

subjects People who are under the control of another

theocracy A government in which the leaders are tied to the church or a specific religion. Leaders rule in the name of a god or gods.

violating Failing to respect

World War II A war fought from 1939 to 1945 in which the United Kingdom, the United States, France, Russia, China, and other countries defeated Germany, Italy, and Japan

FOR MORE INFORMATION

Books

Ganeri, Anita. *Kings & Queens: The History of the British Monarchy*, Haynes Pocket Manual. Newbury Park, CA: Haynes Publishing, 2010.

Harris, Nathaniel. *Monarchy*, Systems of Government. New York: World Almanac Library, 2005.

Hurwitz, Jane. *Monarchy*, Reading Essentials in Social Studies. Logan, IA: Perfection Learning, 2003.

Schiel, Katy. *Monarchy: A Primary Source Analysis*. New York: Rosen Publishing Group, 2003.

Stefoff, Rebecca. *Monarchy*, Political Systems of the World. New York: Benchmark Books, 2007.

Websites

Kidipede: www.historyforkids.org/learn/government/monarchy.htm

Project Britain: projectbritain.com/royal/index.htm

The World of Royalty: www.royalty.nu/history/index.html

INDEX